THE JOURNEY THAT SAVED

Curious  *George*

The True Wartime Escape *of*
Margret and H. A. Rey

by LOUISE BORDEN
illustrated by ALLAN DRUMMOND

HOUGHTON MIFFLIN HARCOURT
BOSTON   NEW YORK

For
Amy Flynn, Emily Linsay, Eleni Beja, and Bethany Vinhateiro...
my fine editors who shared the journey with me...
for
Lay Lee Ong...
and always, for Pete.
— L.B.

For Louise, who made the journey.
— A.D.

Acknowledgments

The names on the list of people who helped me unlock the past and the Reys' wartime experiences are many. Early encouragers were my husband, Pete, Susan Stark, Johanna Hurwitz, and Camilla Warrick. Lay Lee Ong, the executor of the Rey estate, strongly cheered me on. So did Cate Ayars, and Ted Borden, and colleagues in the children's book world: M. K. Kroeger, Cat Smith, Margaret McElderry, Emma Dryden, Ann Bobco, George Ella Lyon, Barb Libby, and Connie Trounstine.

Additional thanks go to the following friends:

The de Grummond Collection: Dee Jones, Ann Ashmore, Ginamarie Pugliese, and Danielle Bishop
Houghton Mifflin: Eden Edwards, Sheila Smallwood, Carol Goldenberg Rosen, Andrea Pinkney, Judy O'Malley
French and German translations: Renée Lowther, Cindy Curchin, Kurt Stark, and David Hunter
Conversations about the Reys: In the United States: Lay Lee Ong, André Schiffrin, Grace Maccarone, Charlotte Zolotow, Lee Bennett Hopkins, Marc Simont, and Leonard Marcus; in London: Pat Schleger
Terrass Hotel: Jean Max Hurand and Jean Luc Binet, whose family has owned and managed the hotel since 1912
Château Feuga: Shelagh and Christopher Stedman, of London and St. Mézard, France, who owned the château at the time of my visit, and Christine Reon, of Lectoure, France
Travels, train routes, and maps: Mary Ann Iemmola
Montmartre, Étampes, Acquebouille, Orléans, Agen, Lectoure, St. Mézard, Castex-Lectourois, Château Feuga: Patty Hegman
Avranches: Cindy Curchin and Fr. Tobie, Abbaye du Mont Saint-Michel
Hamburg and the Hagenbeck Zoo: Klaus Gille
Consulates and train stations in Biarritz, Bayonne, and Hendaye: Pete Borden and Elena Pérez

I would also like to thank Allan Drummond for his wonderful illustrations, and for understanding the vision for this book. Hans and Margret Rey would be very pleased by Allan's fine artistic talent and creative imagination.

Text copyright © 2005 by Louise Borden. Illustrations copyright © 2005 by Allan Drummond.
Back matter © 2016 by Louise Borden.
All rights reserved. For information about permission to reproduce selections from this book,
write to trade.permissions@hmhco.com or to Permissions, Houghton Miflin Harcourt Publishing Company,
3 Park Avenue, 19th Floor, New York, New York 10016.
www.hmhco.com.
The text of this book is set in Bembo, DK Lemon Yellow Sun, Alan, Garamond Narrow and Mona Lisa.
The illustrations are watercolor on paper.
Image credits can be found on page 95.

ISBN: 978-0-544-80033-5 paper over board   ISBN: 978-0-544-76345-6 paperback

Printed in China
SCP 10 9 8 7 6 5 4 3 2
4500654090

CONTENTS

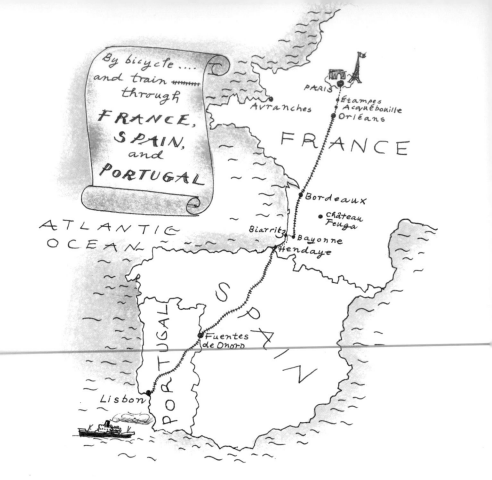

By bicycle.... and train ⊢⊢⊢⊢⊢⊢⊢ through

FRANCE, SPAIN, and PORTUGAL

PARIS
Étampes
Avranches
Acquébouille
Orléans

FRANCE

Bordeaux
Château
Feuga
Biarritz
Bayonne
Hendaye

ATLANTIC OCEAN

SPAIN

PORTUGAL
Fuentes de Oñoro

Lisbon

FINDING THE STORY

For many years, I was intrigued by the story of Margret and H. A. Rey's flight from Paris on bicycles in June 1940. Others in the children's book field had mentioned this escape from the Nazi invasion, but no one seemed to know the details of those harrowing days. The story felt incomplete. I wanted to know more. I wanted real images. I was curious, just like the Reys' famous little monkey, George.

And so I began my own journey, a journey of research. Rich sources for my research were Margret and Hans Rey's personal papers, donated by their estate to the de Grummond Children's Literature Collection at the University of Southern Mississippi. This nationally known library houses the papers and original artwork of more than 1,200 children's book authors and illustrators.

But after sifting through hundreds of the Reys' letters, notebook pages, and photographs, and even after walking through Paris on various research trips, I still had questions without answers. How many kilometers did the Reys travel on those two bicycles? Which roads did they follow on their journey south? What happened to the belongings that they had to leave behind? What wartime dangers did they face?

Over several years I had conversations in person or by phone with people who had known the Reys. I wrote letters and e-mailed people in Germany, England, Portugal, and France. And I traveled to some of the towns, cities, and addresses gleaned from the letters and work diaries that the Reys wrote during 1936–40, the years that they lived in Paris. Each step of the way, I tried to focus on Margret and Hans before *Curious George* was published and brought them fame.

Dates, postmarks, travel papers, and expense records provided invaluable clues in French, English, German, and Portuguese. Newspaper interviews from the 1940s and 1950s gave me needed details. Slowly, piece by piece, I began to stitch together the fabric of their story.

The Journey That Saved Curious George is my way, as a writer, of becoming a witness to part of Hans and Margret Rey's story. It is my way of honoring their creativity and their courage during a dark time in history for many countries of Europe.

Louise Borden

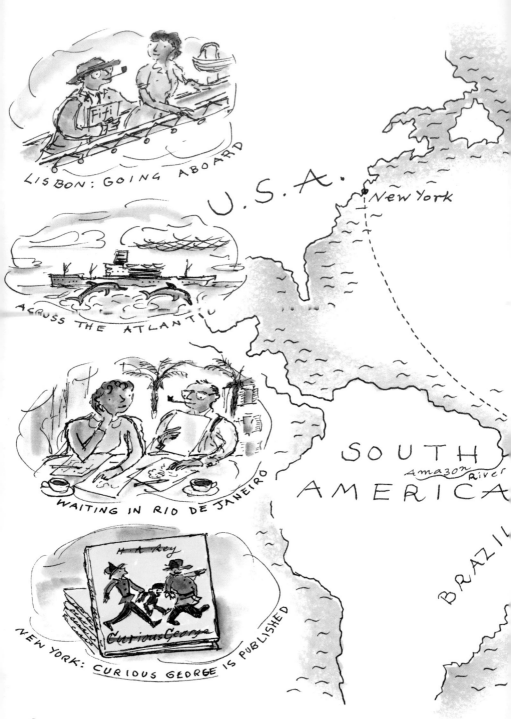

LISBON: GOING ABOARD

ACROSS THE ATLANTIC

WAITING IN RIO DE JANEIRO

NEW YORK: CURIOUS GEORGE IS PUBLISHED

U.S.A.

New York

SOUTH AMERICA

Amazon River

BRAZIL

ATLANTIC

OCEAN

London

GERMANY

Hamburg

Paris

FRANCE

PORTUGAL SPAIN

Lisbon

MADEIRA S.Vicente

AFRICA

the
Sea
Voyage
that saved

Curious George

de

eiro

Above: *H. A. and Margret Rey at a book signing. ca. 1945*

Opposite, left: *H. A. Rey, born September 16, 1898*

Opposite, right: *Margret Rey, born May 16, 1906*

PART 1

TWO ARTISTS

1906 CHILDHOODS IN GERMANY

In 1906, Hans Augusto Reyersbach was a boy growing up in Hamburg, Germany, a port city with canals and a thousand bridges . . . and the River Elbe, which ran to the North Sea.

At the age of eight, Hans spent many hours in the cold breeze near Hamburg's docks, watching foreign ships and barges move along the Elbe. For the rest of his life, Hans would love boats and rivers and the sea.

Above:
Scenes of Hamburg at the beginning of the twentieth century

Often Hans visited the Hagenbeck Zoo with his brother and two sisters. *Monkeys and lions! Polar bears and seals!* The world of animals from faraway places was just a few streets from the Reyersbach home.

It was at this wonderful zoo that Hans learned to imitate the sounds of animals. He could roar like a fierce lion. He could bark like a seal. Another favorite place for young Hans was the circus. All those horses and bright colors! *What a show!*

Hans loved to draw pictures and paint. And he was good at it. Hans made a painting of horses in the park, near one of Hamburg's beautiful lakes. Later, in school, Hans studied Latin and Greek, French and English. He knew five languages, including German.

Top right: *Illustration by H. A. Rey in* Whiteblack the Penguin, *2000*

Bottom right: *Painting by Hans Reyersbach, 1906*

11

Margarete Waldstein, who was born the same year that Hans turned eight, also grew up in Hamburg during those early years of a new century. Like the Reyersbach family, the Waldsteins were Jewish. Margarete and her two brothers and two sisters had a good life, full of comfort and culture and books. Margarete wanted to become an artist. Later she studied art and photography at a school in Germany: the famous Bauhaus.

Street in Hamburg at the turn of the nineteenth century

Top left: *Margarete Waldstein as a young girl*

Top right: *Margarete Waldstein as a toddler*

Bottom: *Margret's certificate of completion for Klosterschule. Official documents show different spellings of her first name.*

Klofterfchule

Zeugnis der Reife.

Fräulein *Margarethe Elisabeth Waldstein*

geboren zu *Altona*

13

The next years were full of change and adventure for Hans
Reyersbach. During World War I, he was a soldier in Kaiser
Wilhelm's German army. Hans didn't like war, and he didn't
like being a soldier. And he was still drawing pictures. Hans
loved to laugh, so sometimes his sketches were quite funny.

On clear nights, he studied the stars and the constellations.
Hans was a deep thinker as well as an artist. Always, he was
curious about the world. Because of his months on the eastern
front, Hans could now speak a smattering of Russian.

Hans Reyersbach as a young German soldier

When Germany lost the war, twenty-year-old Hans Reyersbach went home to Hamburg and found work making posters for the local circus. But times were very hard in his city, and there was little money.

After a few years as a university student, Hans packed his sketchbooks, his paintbrushes, and his pipe and headed to Brazil on a ship.

Sketches by Hans Reyersbach

In 1925, Rio de Janeiro was an exotic city with tall, rugged mountains on one side and the blue sea on the other.

It was a great port of world trade, like Hamburg. Its plazas and streets were swirls of colored tiles. Hans liked to stroll along Copacabana, a wide beach with crowds of bathers and rows of striped umbrellas and tents.

It was hot in Brazil—so Hans wore a broad hat, even in the shade of Rio's palm trees and cafés.

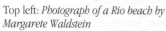

Top left: *Photograph of a Rio beach by Margarete Waldstein*

Illustrations: From Curious George, *1941*

Bottom right: *Poster of Brazilian coffee markets by H. A. Rey*

When he traveled up and down the Amazon River, Hans watched the monkeys and made drawings of them. *Monkeys and more monkeys!* And they weren't in a zoo. They chattered in the branches of trees in the small towns where Hans traveled as he sold bathtubs and kitchen sinks to earn money. Now he was fluent in another language: *Portuguese.*

1935

Nine years after Hans left Hamburg, Adolf Hitler came to power in Germany. Life began to change for the German people, especially for Germans who were Jewish. Margarete Waldstein left Hamburg and worked as a photographer in London. Then in 1935, as Hans had done years earlier, Margarete traveled the long ocean kilometers to Rio de Janeiro. She was looking for new work and adventure, and she knew that Hans Reyersbach, an old family friend whom she admired, was living in Rio.

Adolf Hitler marching with Nazi officials in Berlin, ca. 1933

The two artists began to work together in business, sharing their talents in writing and drawing. Hans was the gentle one. Margarete, with her red hair and artist's spunk, was never afraid to speak her mind. Like Hans, she enjoyed animals and zoos and the circus. Together, they made a great team.

That August, Hans and Margarete were married and they lived together in their Rio apartment with two pet marmosets. Those little monkeys were *always* getting into mischief. During this time, Margarete decided to shorten her name to Margret.

Reyersbach . . . Reyersbach . . . It was a hard name for Brazilians to pronounce. Now that Hans was trying to earn money by drawing and painting large posters and maps, he began to sign his work "H. A. Rey." It was much easier for clients in his new country. And . . . it was a name to remember.

Top right: *Business card drawn by H. A. Rey*
Bottom left: *Poster by H. A. Rey*

A Hotel in Paris

Months later, as Brazilian citizens with Brazilian passports, the Reys began a honeymoon trip to Europe and took their Rio pets with them. It was a cold, rainy crossing to England. Margret knitted sweaters to keep the tiny monkeys warm, but, even so, the marmosets didn't survive the journey.

After visiting several cities, Hans and Margret ended up at the

Terrass Hotel
12, rue Joseph de Maistre
Paris.

From Curious George, *1941*

From Curious George, *1941*

The Reys planned to stay at this hotel for two weeks because it was in Montmartre, the neighborhood of Paris that was famous for the many artists who had lived there. Beautiful Paris was elegant and exciting. It seemed to be just the right city for Hans and Margret, so the Terrass Hotel became their home for the next four years.

From Katy No-Pocket, *1944*

The Terrass had two large buildings, one with guest rooms and one with apartments. The Reys took an apartment on the fifth floor, number 505. Pets were allowed at the hotel, so for a few years Hans and Margret had two French turtles to keep them company: Claudia and Claudius.

In every season, Hans and Margret looked
across the rooftops and chimney pots.
What a view! They never grew tired of seeing
the graceful Eiffel Tower etched against the
blue or gray Paris sky.

From their windows in 505, the Reys could hear the flutter of pigeons on the balcony ledge and, down below, the quick rumble of taxis on the rue de Maistre. Just across the street in the cemetery was a spooky jumble of vaults, graves, and tombstones, dark with the soot of the city.

Opposite top: *The Eiffel Tower, 1930s*
Opposite bottom: *Paris photograph of H. A. Rey taken by Margret Rey*

The Reys' neighborhood,
Montmartre, was really an old village
on the highest hill of the city, with
vineyards, stray cats, and the windmill
of the famed Moulin Rouge cabaret.
Steep cobblestone streets wound
up, and up, and up to Sacre Coeur,
a landmark church with gleaming
white domes.

The Reys sketched and photographed the fishermen along the banks of the Seine, the captains and their families who lived on the local barges, the booksellers on the quays who, each morning, unlocked their wooden boxes and sold secondhand books to those who passed by . . . and, of course, the animals at the zoo.

Often, Hans and Margret walked to their favorite cafés for lunch or dinner. They sat at sidewalk tables with their friends, drank cups of strong coffee, and talked about their creative ideas as they watched the world move by.

Four Paris photographs taken by Margret Rey, 1939–40

During these years, Hans and Margret began writing and illustrating their books for children. Margret was a good critic for Hans's drawings. The Reys worked with several publishers in Paris and another one in London. They exchanged detailed letters with their editors about their new projects.

Above left: *Interior art from* Cecily G. and the 9 Monkeys

Above right: *Letters from the Reys' British and French publishers*

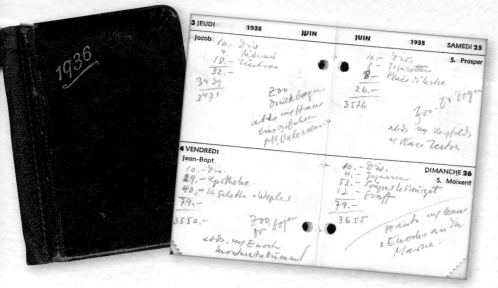

The years were carefully recorded by Hans. Each day, he jotted down the places he and Margret visited, living expenses, and notes about his work. He filled page after page of his pocket calendar with his small, penciled script, writing words in French, English, and German. Then he added up the monthly expenses in French francs.

In 1939, a wonderful new manuscript was in progress: a story about a monkey named Fifi who had appeared in one of Hans's first books. Now Fifi would be the star of his own book, *The Adventures of Fifi.* Fifi was a very *curious* little monkey—he was always getting into trouble and then finding a way to get out of it.

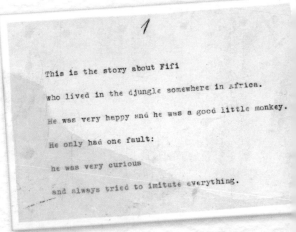

1

This is the story about Fifi

who lived in the djungle somewhere in africa.

He was very happy and he was a good little monkey.

He only had one fault:

he was very curious

and always tried to imitate everything.

Top: H. A. Rey's 1936 diary from June 1938
Right: Early manuscript page

1939 WAR BEGINS

On September 1, 1939, war began in Europe. The battles were far away—in Poland. Still, many Parisians left the city until times seemed more secure. That week, Margret and Hans packed their valises and took a long train ride southwest to a remote village in the French countryside. They spent the next four months at Château Feuga, owned by friends. Its walls and towers were more than five hundred years old.

German invasion of Poland, September 1939

Inset: *Photograph of Château Feuga taken in 1939 by Margret Rey*

Opposite:
From Whiteblack the Penguin, *2000*

Up . . . up . . . round and round . . . Hans climbed the creaky, narrow stairs to a square room in the largest of Feuga's three towers. He pushed open the heavy shutters and smelled the fresh September air. Far to the south was a smudge of mountains: the Pyrenées! This simple room was the perfect place for a studio where Hans could work on his book illustrations. Or read, or sit at his desk and think and daydream as he often liked to do.

From Château Feuga it was an hour's walk to the closest post office, but still the Reys wrote and mailed letters to their publishers. Besides  *The Adventures of Fifi,* Hans and Margret began working on another book—this one about a penguin named Whiteblack, who loved to travel and see the world.

German troops marching
to the Polish front, 1939

But since September, France had been at war with Germany, and the Reys had German accents when they spoke French. A few local people whispered among themselves and called a village police officer, who then paid a visit to Feuga. Were these château guests perhaps German spies? Hans led the officer up the stairs to his studio.

The scattered pages of sketches and words, and watercolor illustrations of Fifi, the little monkey, and Whiteblack, the penguin, told  the true story: Hans and Margret created books for children.

Above: *Two illustrations from* Curious George, *1941*
Right: *From* Whiteblack the Penguin, *2000*

In 1939, Hitler's Germany was not a safe place for Jewish people to live. Hans and Margret worried about old friends still living in Hamburg. Their own families had moved away to London or Rio, and the Reys were glad to be living in France, glad they had become Brazilian citizens while in South America. Brazil was a neutral country in the brewing conflict in Europe.

In December, it was cold and drafty in the tower studio, too cold to open the shutters. There was snow on the peaks of the Pyrénées. Hans carried his artwork downstairs, and he and Margret packed up their belongings.

The war was still far away, not yet in France. It was safe to return home to the Terrass.

Top right: *From* Whiteblack the Penguin, *2000*
Above: *Card made for Margret Rey by H. A. Rey, December 24, 1939*

THE WINTER OF 1940

That January the Reys were back in their Paris apartment. The streets and cafés seemed bustling and noisy after the quiet months at Feuga. But Hans and Margret loved the energy of the city. Hans completed the title page for *The Adventures of Fifi*: a picture of Fifi in a tree at the zoo, holding the string of a red balloon. Then he signed the illustration in small black letters:

H. a. Rey–Paris Jan. 1940

Hans was also hard at work in apartment 505 painting the watercolors for *Whiteblack the Penguin*. One morning he dipped his brush into some black paint. In two of the illustrations Hans lettered the name PEGGY, his nickname for Margret, on a fishing boat. After all, the Reys were a team.

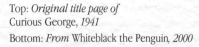

Top: *Original title page of Curious George, 1941*
Bottom: *From* Whiteblack the Penguin, *2000*

On his tiny calendar, Hans recorded the work days as they slipped by:

Penguin . . .
Penguin . . .
Penguin . . .

He studied the illustrations of this new story. *Hmm.* He liked them as much as those for *The Adventures of Fifi.* Perhaps . . . even better. Hans carefully painted a tiny French flag on the stern of Whiteblack's ship. The Reys hoped to go on a ship soon themselves, to America for a visit in April. But it was difficult to leave Europe now because of wartime regulations.

Top: *From Whiteblack the Penguin,* 2000

Bottom: *H. A. Rey's diary pages from January 1940*

Margret's older brother, also named Hans, came to Paris that winter for a visit. The winter of 1940 was the coldest anyone could remember. Now there was snow on the balcony ledge and on the high walls of the cemetery. Hans Rey the artist and Hans Waldstein, a soldier in the French army, stood together in the cold sunshine on the roof garden of the Terrass while Margret snapped their pictures.

Photographs taken by Margret Rey, 1940

WORKING BY THE SEA

During the windy days of March, Hans worked hard on some final touches for *Fifi*. Then, in April, the Reys packed their suitcases for a train trip to Avranches, a town on the far edge of Normandy, on the English Channel. Now Hans and Margret could enjoy the sea air and look across the wide bay to the ancient fortress Mont St. Michel, a castle built on a rock in the shallow tidal flats.

Would *Fifi* and *Whiteblack* ever become published books? Because of the war, there were now strict laws about printing. Typesetters had joined the army. Paper was getting scarce. Hans mailed letters to editors in London and Paris and included the Reys' vacation address.

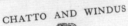

CHATTO AND WINDUS

Partners
HAROLD RAYMOND
I. M. PARSONS
JOHN McDOUGALL

Telegrams:
Telephone
TEMPLE BAR 0137/9

PUBLISHERS
40-42 WILLIAM IV STREET
LONDON
W.C.2

6th March, 1940.

HR/HGA

Dear Mr. Rey,

Very many thanks for your letter of March 1st. The MS. of "Whiteblack" arrived a few hours later. Everyone who has seen it is as delighted as usual with your work. Some even prefer it as a whole to "Fifi", but I rather fancy that a person's judgment over these two books would ultimately depend on whether he happened to prefer a penguin to a monkey. Personally I slightly prefer "Fifi". He went straight to my heart. On the other hand many people dislike all monkeys, and as everyone likes and is amused by penguins, possibly "Whiteblack" might sell better.

The postponement of your trip to America will make it even more difficult for you to make up your mind what to do, but I am in no two minds about what I would advise you to do. I am convinced that your only hope of earning money out of these books is to put your trust completely in some English publisher – Chatto's or someone else – and take a chance that it will turn out well for you. Every English publisher is in the same position as ourselves in that he cannot import sheets of a juvenile either from the U.S.A. or from France. Also I am convinced that no English publisher would undertake the printing of "Fifi" or of "Whiteblack" unless he was sure of selling at least half his edition to America. To print those books solely for the British Empire market is not a practical proposition.

I suggest, therefore, that your wisest course would be to send us back the MS. of "Fifi" and let us send both that and "Whiteblack" to Stokes, together with a quotation based on the estimates which we have got for "Fifi". I ought to mention that for the 1/9d. I stated in my last letter you should now read 1/9d. owing to a mistake on the part of the printer. If this price is altogether higher than they can pay, it is for them to say whether they would like to receive revised estimates.

H. A. Rey
Hotel D'Angleterre
Avranches (Manche)

Top: *Mont Saint-Michel*
Bottom: *Editorial letter from the Reys' British publisher*

The Reys were relieved when Hans signed a contract for *Fifi*, as well as for two small manuscripts, and received an advance of money from their Paris publisher. Little did they know how needed those French francs would be in the weeks to follow.

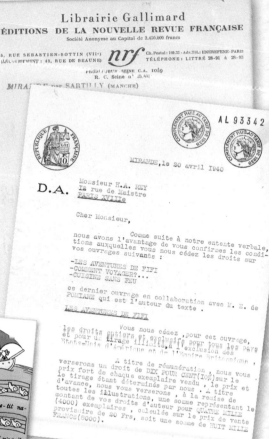

Margret and Hans began a new project: a book of nursery songs in French and English. Hans drew the strong black lines of his style and added the musical notes. In wartime, children needed good books and songs more than ever.

Top right: *H. A. Rey's contract with French publisher Gallimard*
Middle and bottom: *Two pages from H. A. Rey's* Au Claire de la Lune *and Other French Nursery Songs, 1941*

THE TERRIBLE WEEK

On the morning of May 10, 1940, while Hans was again at his desk, touching up a page of *Fifi*, history was happening. Kilometers away from Avranches, the German army crossed over the border into the neutral countries of Holland, Belgium, and Luxembourg.

Dutch street in May 1940

That day Hans bought two local newspapers. In the cafés, people listened intently to the radio broadcasts of the rapid German advance. Everyone was worried. Some had sons or brothers fighting with the French army. But, the French army was strong! It was mighty! It would protect Avranches… and all of France! It would stop the advance of the Germans.

Right and opposite, top: *H. A. Rey's diary pages from May 1940*

That terrible week, it was
hard for Hans and Margret
to put their hearts into their
work. France was their
home now. On May 13,
Hans wrote in his diary:

*Songs English
very slowly because
of the events.*

The war was no longer far
away. On the northern
French border, the Nazi tanks moved like lightning.
It was a *blitzkrieg!*

On May 19, Hans recorded *Songs* in his notebook. It would be
the last day that H. A. Rey painted his book illustrations in France.
From then on, he and Margret needed
to focus on their safety in the time of war.
They bought train tickets to return home.

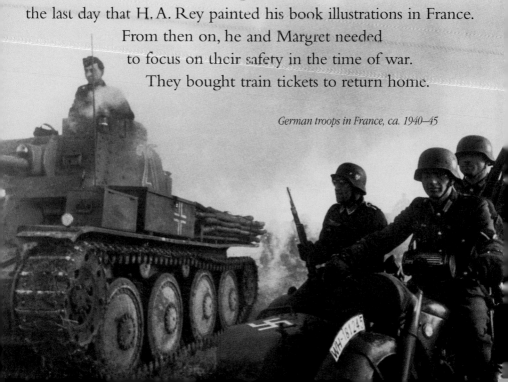

German troops in France, ca. 1940–45

PART 2

ESCAPE FROM PARIS

On May 23, the Reys arrived
back in Paris and took the metro
to Montmartre. The cafés were still
open and busy, but the tempo of
the city had changed.

From the north came a stream
of refugees—more and more arrived
in Paris each day. Hundreds... then
thousands... then thousands more.
Train stations were filled with people.
Such anxious faces and so few trains!
Everyone wanted to travel in the same
direction: *south* ... away from the fighting.
There was not enough food or water at
the stations. In the unusual June heat, some
refugees fainted.

The elegant avenues of the French capital
were crowded with bicycles, Belgian farm
carts and horses, and Dutch cars with
mattresses strapped to the roof. All belonged
to civilians fleeing from the war zones to
the north. Even barges on the Seine carried
refugees. The stories in the Paris newspapers
were full of gloomy news.

43

Plans to Flee

At their Terrass apartment, Hans and Margret remained calm. But they were German-born Jews, and Hitler's soldiers were moving swiftly toward the French capital. The Reys would have to leave, and quickly.

They decided to try to return to Brazil, and then travel on to America. Margret's sister was there, near New York City. But there was much to do before they could leave. One needed *so many papers* to leave a country in a time of war. *Identity cards. Visas.* And *tickets.* Tickets for any trains heading south. And *money!* One always needed money for a long journey . . . Would they get it all in time?

The next day, Hans went immediately to the Brazilian consulate and paid for updated passports. He withdrew money from his bank accounts, as many francs as he was allowed. That week, the Reys went to the same few places over and over again to get the documents they needed for their journey: the American consulate ...
the Portuguese consulate ...
the Spanish consulate ... and again, the bank. Then back to the consulates.

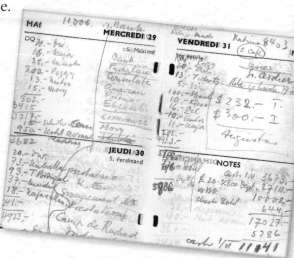

Everywhere they went for their documents, there were long queues that wound around street corners. *Thump-thump! Thump-thump!* Everything needed to be official. Everything needed to be stamped with the date.

The list of expenses in Hans's notebook grew and grew:

    baggage ...
       insurance ...
          taxi ...
             tailor ...
                umbrella ...

Hans's calendar became a record of a husband and wife, two artists, getting ready to leave their beloved home.

Opposite, top: *H. A. Rey's Brazilian passport*
Opposite, bottom: *Pages from the Reys' French identity cards*
Above: *H. A. Rey's diary pages from May 1940*

45

At night, the streets of Paris had an eerie dark blue gleam from the blackout cloth on the streetlamps. The slow, loud whine of air raid sirens, mostly false alarms, woke the city night after night. The news from the front was grim. The Belgian king had surrendered to the Germans. Most of the British army, and more than 100,000 French soldiers, had to be rescued from the beaches at Dunkirk. The English Channel was full of hundreds of boats and ships trying to save the retreating armies, taking them to safety in England.

On June 7, Hans recorded in his notebook that the neighborhood was awakened in the night by an alert from the *préfecture*.

CAFÉ

BON VIN

By June 10, two million Parisians had left the city, including the government officials who fled first to Tours, and then farther south to Bordeaux. Only one newspaper was still being printed in Paris. Monuments and historic buildings were ringed with sandbags as protection against bombs and fighting. Shops were shuttered. Taxis were impossible to find.

A belated radio broadcast let citizens know that Paris had been declared an open city. The government had decided not to barricade its streets or fight the invading army, whose tanks could turn the French capital into rubble in a matter of days. Major avenues and the lovely, wide Champs-Élysées were empty. Paris was waiting . . .

A Bicycle Maker

Hans and Margret were among the few tenants still at the Terrass Hotel. On June 11, the Reys went scouting for two bicycles to buy since they had no car, and the trains were no longer running. They found a small shop open, but the owner shrugged and pointed to a tandem *vélo*. It was the only bicycle left in his store. "You should have come sooner, monsieur." Hans wheeled the long bicycle outside and persuaded Margret to practice riding it with him on the rue de la Paix and around the Place Vendôme. It was a disaster!

Let's go!

Ready?

Ring Ring!

VELO Bicyclette

Margret shook her head and said that riding a tandem would *never* work. The Reys returned the bicycle and bargained with the owner. For 1,600 francs, almost a month's lodging at the Terrass, Hans bought four large baskets, and spare parts for two bicycles from the shelves of the *vélo* store. Margret hurried back to their apartment and chose a small pile of belongings. She took the Reys' manuscripts and artwork from the desk and slid them carefully into a satchel.

Meanwhile, Hans worked in the back room of the store, with tools, handlebars, pedals, and tires. With baskets on each bicycle, the Reys would be able to pack a few more things for their journey. Then Hans recorded his work in his pocket calendar. That hot June afternoon, H. A. Rey, the artist, became a bicycle maker.

The biggest adventure of his life was about to begin . . .

Look out!

Pedal!

Rrring!

BEEP!

HOOT!

Pedaling South

On Wednesday, June 12, it was raining on the empty streets of Paris. *Finally* raining, after the days of hot weather. At five-thirty in the morning, the Reys began their flight from the city, across wet cobblestone streets that glistened beneath their tires.

The Reys had to travel light: only a few clothes and their winter coats, some bread and cheese, a little meat, water, an umbrella, Hans's pipe, and the precious manuscripts, including *The Adventures of Fifi*. Everything else they owned was left behind. Hans hoped the boxes and suitcases at the Terrass would somehow be shipped safely to Margret's sister in America as planned.

Hans and Margret joined the thousands of refugees leaving Paris. After the first kilometers, the Reys' clothes were damp with rain so Hans made sure that his artwork stayed dry in the basket under his winter coat. Hans and Margret rode in and out of the lines of cars, taxis and trucks, green city buses and farm carts, other bicycles and stragglers on foot.

The drizzle of rain stopped
and the sun came out.
The Reys pedaled . . .
and pedaled . . . and pedaled.
With each kilometer, the seats of
their *vélos* felt harder on their backsides.
Their necks and their backs began to ache.
And their legs and their knees. Even the palms of their hands.

Everywhere there was confusion and noise: grinding gears of overheated cars and the frightening drone of German scout planes. Constant and relentless were the car horns, honking to speed up the crawling procession of the largest motorized evacuation in history.

More than five million people were on the roads of France that day. Among this sea of humanity were two small figures:
    Margret and H. A. Rey.

Help Along The Way

Margret and Hans were not afraid. They felt a sense of freedom, traveling light. Most important, they were together.

That first day, the Reys pedaled forty-eight kilometers to the town of Étampes. Past the crowded main square, they found a farmhouse set back from the road. The owner offered Margret and Hans simple lodging: a room already housing a servant and a woman refugee. The grateful Reys wrapped themselves in their coats and instantly fell asleep.

By three o'clock the next morning, Margret and Hans
were on their way again in the darkness. The sky was
a blue-black canvas filled with stars. As the sun rose,
the road flattened out into open land. That day, Hans and
Margret pedaled twenty-six kilometers until they reached the
tiny village of Acquebouille. They spied a farm on a side road
and walked their bicycles into a walled yard full of thick mud
and clucking hens. Once again, the Reys were lucky.
A kindly farmwoman offered them sweet, fresh milk
as well as a place to sleep. Hans recorded the route
and events:

Nuit au etable aux Vaches..

That night, Hans and Margret Rey slept
on a bed of hay in a stable full of cows.

H. A. Rey's June 1940 diary pages, written in French

Early the next day, the Reys
were off again, pedaling, pedaling, thirty-two
kilometers from Acquebouille to the city of
Orléans. There Hans and Margret hoped to catch
a train that would take them south. They still had
far to go: their destination was Portugal . . . and then . . .
a ship across the Atlantic.

The train station in Orléans was bedlam! There were hand-
lettered signs for missing children, tacked up on the walls by
frantic parents:

Jean-Claude Moncourt, 5 ans,
perdu le 10 juin.

Helene et Martine Landau . . .
6 et 4 ans—perdu pres d'ici le 11 juin.

These were difficult days for the French people. Two days
after the Reys passed through, Étampes was heavily
bombed. Their escape had been narrow indeed.

56

57

At the Orléans station, Hans touched his inside pocket, checking that the documents and tickets he had bought in Paris were safe. Then he and Margret hoisted their bicycles and dusty bundles into the crowded train car headed in the direction of Bordeaux. The train slowly pulled out of the Orléans station, then swayed and clattered along the tracks as it gathered speed. To Hans and Margret, after three days of pedaling, the sound was wonderful.

The date was Friday, June 14, 1940, a terrible day in the history of Paris: Nazi troops had goose-stepped by the thousands down the broad Champs-Élysées and

replaced the French flag flying atop the Eiffel Tower
with the swastika of Hitler's Third Reich.

Occupied Paris was only 106 kilometers to the north. Safety
for the Reys lay in the long journey ahead. Margret and Hans
dozed and talked as they watched two days and two nights
cover the landscape. Hans jotted down the direction of their
route in his diary as he sat with Margret by the open windows
hour after hour. The air was hot inside the train.

What had happened to Paris and the Terrass Hotel?
Were their other friends safe?

So many questions without answers.

WEARY REFUGEES

Finally, close to five a.m. on June 16, the Reys' train pulled into the station at Bayonne. Hans and Margret, tired and disheveled, climbed down to the platform and pushed their bicycles through the crowds of people, inhaling the air of southern France. What a clamor of station noise! *But what a relief!*

The population of the small town was triple its usual size. Local police pointed them in the direction of the public high school. That night, after being welcomed with plates of good food, Hans and Margret curled up again on their winter coats, surrounded by hundreds of other weary refugees.

The next morning, Hans counted up their remaining francs.
The amount was shrinking, day by day. The Reys bought only
a few things: soap, shirts, two jackets, a shawl, and a backpack.
Hans sent telegrams to London and Rio, telling family and
friends that they had gotten out of Paris.

The Reys left Bayonne and bicycled down the coast to nearby
Biarritz to get more travel visas. Outside the Portuguese
consulate in the shade of the tamarind trees, Hans and
Margret waited in line for four hours. Those who couldn't get
permission to travel through Spain or Portugal would have to
remain in occupied France for the duration of the war.

Finally, Margret and Hans were granted their transit visas! They would be allowed to travel on to Hendaye, the French border town a few kilometers south. There they would need approval to board the train for Spain. Others, ahead of them and behind them in line, were not so fortunate.

That night, in Hendaye, the Reys spread out their coats on the floor of a small restaurant. With a handful of francs, they had persuaded a waiter to let them spend the night there. The next morning, at the Spanish consulate, their wait was five hours. Then . . . finally . . . a weary Spanish official stamped the Reys' papers. *Thump! Thump!* Margret and Hans celebrated by eating a lunch of sardines and tuna fish. Now they could travel through Spain and on to Portugal.

And the two bicycles that had carried the Reys all those kilometers out of Paris? Hans sold them on the train platform to a customs official for 650 francs. The Reys would not be needing them in Lisbon, or onboard a ship to America.

ACROSS SPAIN

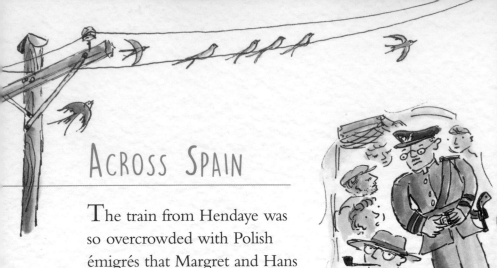

The train from Hendaye was
so overcrowded with Polish
émigrés that Margret and Hans
had to stand in the swaying car
before they could find seats.
An official passed slowly through
their car, checking identity papers with stern eyes.
He began to question Hans about his job and asked
Hans to open up his leather satchel. Perhaps these
passengers were spies, leaving France with important
papers?

Then the official thumbed through the pages of
The Adventures of Fifi. *"Ah . . . un livre pour les enfants."*

The official smiled briefly. He handed the passports and visas back to Hans and moved on. Once again, the mischievous little monkey had rescued the Reys.

Hans and Margret Rey had been on the run for nine days. For two more days, the train chugged across Spain, past olive groves and open plains to the border town of Fuentes de Oñoro. During the long customs check, Hans was glad that he still had some money in his pocket when the local clerks demanded inflated fees in pesetas. Finally the train crossed into Portugal.

WAITING IN LISBON

On Sunday, June 23, at one-thirty in the afternoon, Margret and Hans Rey arrived in Lisbon. The neutral capital had suddenly become "the city of refugees." Lisbon was now the safe haven for diplomats, and a temporary destination for thousands of others who were trying to leave Europe on one of the ships in the harbor.

Somehow, despite the crowds, the Reys found a hotel room.
A real bed . . . with pillows and clean sheets. And a bathtub with
hot water.

"Wonderful!

And much too good!"

Hans wrote in his pocket diary.
Both of the Reys were asleep before nine that night.

*H. A. Rey's June 23, 1940, diary page,
written in French and German*

Right away the next morning they
made phone calls, wrote letters to family and friends,
and sent a telegram to their bank in Rio:

have had a very narrow escape
Baggage all lost
have not sufficient money in hand

While waiting for passage on a ship, the Reys' address for
the next month was a few blocks from the straw-colored
Tagus River:

Rua do Ferregial de Baixo 33.

After money was wired to their bank in Lisbon, Hans and
Margret were able to shop for pajamas and other essential
things, as well as paper and paints. The two artists were safe in
neutral Portugal, but other parts of France, in addition to Paris,
were now under the dark shadow of German occupation.

Top: *Telegram sent by H. A. Rey from Lisbon; visa stamp, July 15, 1940*
Opposite, top: *Bank receipt;* opposite, bottom: *letters to editors written by the Reys from Lisbon*

For many Europeans, the war years of terror and fear were just beginning.

On July 15, Margret and Hans had their required vaccination papers signed and stamped. Once again they began to pack their belongings. Far across the Atlantic was Rio . . . their next steppingstone to a new life in America.

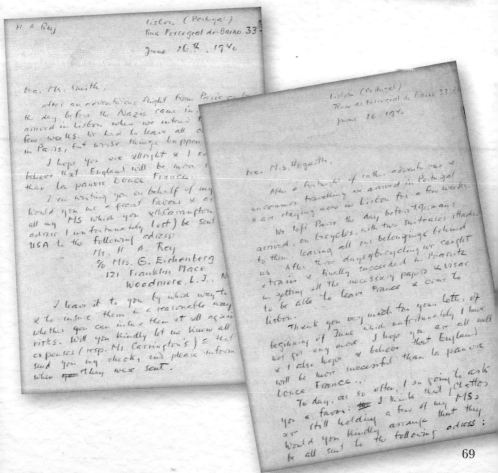

An Ocean Voyage

On July 21, Hans and Margret walked up the gangplank of the *Angola,* carrying their luggage and first-class tickets for a thirteen-day passage to South America. The wide bow of the *Angola* cut through the dark blue swells of the Atlantic as the steamship, crowded with refugees, headed out to sea. It docked briefly at Vicente, a town on the Portuguese island of Madeira, and then sailed southwest toward Rio.

Each morning, the Reys could see the sun come up over the ocean from the small porthole in their stateroom. Almost all of the passengers on the *Angola* had fled from their homes because of the war. All had stories to tell at their tables in the dining room. When the *Angola* rolled and pitched in rough weather, the plates and silverware slid sideways with a clatter.

Passenger list of Angola

Lisbon

Vicente, Madeira

Rio de Janeiro

Brazil

New ideas

71

WAITING IN RIO

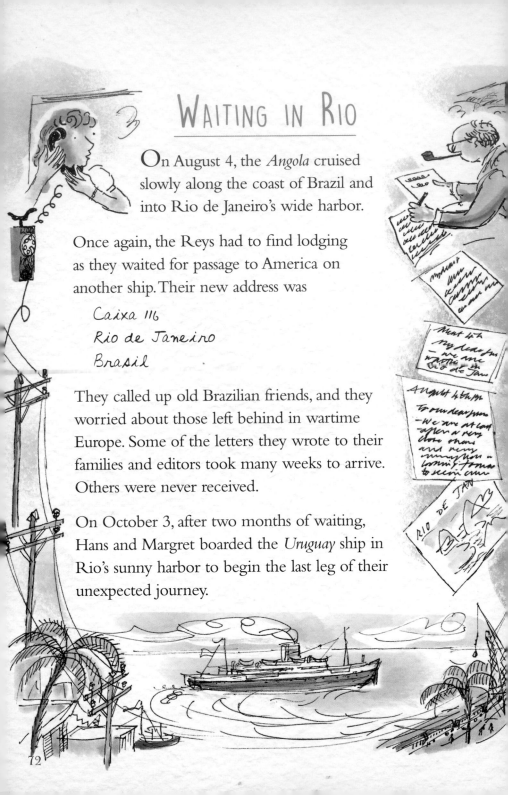

On August 4, the *Angola* cruised slowly along the coast of Brazil and into Rio de Janeiro's wide harbor.

Once again, the Reys had to find lodging as they waited for passage to America on another ship. Their new address was

Caixa 116
Rio de Janeiro
Brasil

They called up old Brazilian friends, and they worried about those left behind in wartime Europe. Some of the letters they wrote to their families and editors took many weeks to arrive. Others were never received.

On October 3, after two months of waiting, Hans and Margret boarded the *Uruguay* ship in Rio's sunny harbor to begin the last leg of their unexpected journey.

One clear night, they took
a late evening stroll on the windy deck.
What bright stars! The ocean sky was like a
huge blackboard dotted with tiny lights. All
Hans needed was a stick of celestial chalk
to connect these Atlantic stars
and map his favorite constellations.

A New Home

On October 14, 1940, four months
after they bicycled out of Paris, the
Reys saw the New York City skyline
framed by a blue sky and brilliant sunshine.
Their ship followed the wake of a sturdy
tugboat into New York Harbor. Passengers
began to point and cheer. There, ahead, was
the Statue of Liberty, the landmark
of freedom given to America
in friendship by the country
of France.

Margret and Hans leaned against the ship railing and pulled up their collars, facing the cold, steady breeze. An unknown future in the United States lay ahead for the two artists. Like Fifi, the mischievous monkey whose book of adventures they had carried in a bicycle basket, Hans and Margret Rey had had a narrow escape from wartime Paris. But the Reys had talent and enough energy to climb mountains if they had to, in creating new books.

That chilly October day in New York Harbor, Hans, Margret, and Fifi were on their way . . . to a new home, on another continent, with stories to tell.

Just a year later, their first book would be published in America, a book that would bring all three of them enduring fame and affection throughout the world. Like Hans Reyersbach and Margarete Waldstein, the little French monkey Fifi would change his name, and it would become one to remember . . . the well-loved Curious George.

After the Escape

Paris remained occupied by German troops until its liberation on August 25, 1944. Nine months after arriving in the United States in October 1940, the Reys received the belongings they had packed up in Paris, including their publishing contracts and correspondence. No one knows how their luggage was shipped from France.

Margret and Hans lived for the next twenty-three years in New York City. They led modest lives, surrounded by books and their pet cocker spaniels. In November 1940, a new editor at Houghton Mifflin, Grace Hogarth, offered the Reys a contract for four books. The Reys had known Grace when she was a children's book editor at their British publisher, Chatto and Windus. Like Margret and Hans, she had also left Europe because of the wartime dangers. The contract included the manuscripts for *The Adventures of Fifi* (eventually retitled *Curious George*), *Raffy and the 9 Monkeys* (retitled *Cecily G. and the 9 Monkeys*), and two lift-the-flap books, *How Do You Get There?* and *Anybody at Home?* Margret and Hans carried all of these with them when they biked out of Paris.

Curious George was published August 17, 1941. The series of books it inspired has sold over seventy-five million copies and been translated into twenty-five languages. The book of nursery songs that the Reys worked on while in Avranches was published in 1941 by Greystone Press. It was displayed in a bookstore window on New York's Fifth Avenue to celebrate the hope for international peace. *Whiteblack the Penguin* wasn't published until

2000, when Anita Silvey, who was then publisher of Houghton Mifflin Children's Books, rediscovered it in the Rey archives.

On April 8, 1946, Margret and Hans Rey became United States citizens. In later years, the Reys built a summer home in Waterville Valley, New Hampshire, where Hans set up his telescope to view the stars and night skies. In 1963 they moved from New York to Cambridge, Massachusetts. Margret and Hans had no children of their own, but their pictures and words have brought joy to millions of young readers around the world.

H. A. Rey died in Boston on August 26, 1977, at the age of seventy-eight. His beloved "Peggy," cared for by a trusted friend, Lay Lee Ong, lived to celebrate her ninetieth birthday. Until her death on December 21, 1996, in Cambridge, Margret continued to be a strong voice and guardian for the Reys' texts and illustrations, and for the mischievous monkey George. The humor and truth in their books continue to charm and inspire us.

A Conversation with

LOUISE BORDEN

Why did you decide to write this book?

I was intrigued by the snippets of information I knew about the Reys' escape from Paris. I had just finished writing a book, *The Little Ships,* about the same time period, June 1940. I wanted to know more details about the Reys' lives as artists, why they were living in Paris, the particulars of their journey. *How far did they bicycle each day? What happened to the belongings they left behind? What was it like to be German-born Jews during this time in Europe?*

How did your audience affect your description of the situation of Jews in France in 1940?

Whenever I'm writing about a European setting during World War II, I try to make the time period accessible to young American readers. It's a real challenge with a subject as complicated as World War II. I think maps can give young readers important information about where events occurred. For *The Journey That Saved Curious George,* I knew many readers might not be aware of the situation in France in 1940. The war was unfolding on many fronts. Armies were in retreat. Governments were surrendering. Imagine the confusion and fright that must have been common among ordinary citizens. So I tried to set the wartime scene by mentioning faraway battles in Poland, then the situation in Denmark and Norway, and, on May 10, the invasion of Holland, Belgium, Luxembourg, and France. All

French citizens were at risk, not just Jews. Everyone was fleeing from the battles.

In 1940, the full implications of what the Germans had in mind for Jewish citizens in France was not yet known by the public. Besides their Brazilian passports, the Reys also held French identity cards that stated their occupation and nationality but not their religion. If the Reys had remained in France, even though their Brazilian passports did not state that they were Jewish, I'm sure they would have been caught in the closing net of the Nazis and been deported to a concentration camp. Within months of the fall of France, foreign Jews were required to be registered on French government lists. Many non-Jewish citizens were deported as well, after Germany took control of France. In my text, I tried to inform readers that Germany was not a safe place for Jews in the 1930s. Many students know about the plight of Jews during World War II and have beginning knowledge of the Holocaust. The story about the Reys takes place before those terrible events unfolded.

What was one thing that surprised you during your research and travels?

As I read through copies of letters and studied the Reys' personal photographs, as well as photos of Paris during this time period, it seemed like a very gray and black-and-white world. Photos were not in color. Newsreels were not in color. Letters were typed or written in black ink on white paper. And yet when I looked at the artwork of Hans Rey, the colors were vibrant—yellow and blue, red and green. And I knew that the Reys' childhoods and their later life in Paris and as refugees were lived in full color. Before I visited Château Feuga, where the Reys spent the fall of 1939, I'd been picturing the black-and-white photo we found in the archives. But when I saw the house it was in full color. This, I think, is what surprised me—the black-and-white research versus the full-color scenes from my travels.

Something else that surprised me: Hans's meticulous notes in his calendar books. He was certainly a man of habit in his record keeping, which seems to be at odds with the image of a typical artist. Hans had an interest in science and philosophy and had planned to study medicine in his university years, but the poor economy in Germany made that impossible. In letters and documents, his small handwriting was neat and orderly, whereas Margret's script appeared much larger and bolder and was sometimes difficult to read.

What do you think accounts for the popularity of Curious George?

I think most people need and love humor in life. The antics and expressions of the character Curious George hit the mark in delighting readers of many ages and nationalities. Think of all the laughter and smiles around the world that have been generated by this one mischievous little monkey! George brings a positive outlook to his readers in those moments when they are turning the pages of his books—an outlook they can carry with them into their own lives.

So many of George's instincts are universal ones. His most famous trait, curiosity, shines through all the Curious George stories and inspires children in what they already know about the world—that it's a big place full of unknown adventures. George also touches our hearts in a unique and special way. He endures through generations of readers because we can each see a part of ourselves in his antics, mishaps, and solutions to comical and unexpected situations.

Does George remind you of Hans and Margret Rey at all?

Yes. I think Hans and Margret live on via the wonderful personality of their famous George. Just by reading the Reys' letters to their family and their editors, I instantly recognized their humor and playful approach to life. Even when they were living under threatening circumstances, their humor and positive energy shone through like a bright thread.

Many scenes in the Curious George books reflect parts of the Reys' lives—just look for a camera, hanging on the wall in a ship cabin, and you'll be reminded that Margret Rey was a photographer. Hans smoked a pipe, just like the Man with the Yellow Hat. Turtles, the zoo scenes, the balloon man—these all came from the Reys' lives in Europe. When I page through the Curious George books, I feel as if I am reliving some of their adventures. Both Margret and Hans were creative and curious people—they explored life with their inquisitive minds. They were always learning new things, and they stepped out into a busy world with a smile, just like George.

Become a DETECTIVE

When I was in sixth grade, my teacher, Mrs. Resor, wrote on my report card, "I think Louise will enjoy research all her life. Bon Voyage!" I was lucky to have such a wise teacher.

When I do research for a book, I become a detective. I look for clues, fit them together to solve the puzzle, and choose the best facts to include in the text. Read on to learn about the clues I used to write *The Journey That Saved Curious George* and how you can be a detective of history too.

Four Clues

Clue 1

CHÂTEAU FEUGA

While paging through documents and photos in the Rey archives at the de Grummond Collection in Hattiesburg, Mississippi, I found this address on letters to and from the Reys:

Monsieur H. A. Rey, Château Feuga, CASTEX-LECTOUROIS.

H. A. Rey at Château Feuga, taken by Margret

The letters were sent soon after France went to war with Germany. I was curious. Did Château Feuga still exist? If so, where was it?

I did my research from 1999 to 2002, before there was Google. So how did I get my information? I contacted people in France, and looked at maps of the region near Castex-Lectourois. Carrying copies of photos taken by Margret Rey, I flew to Paris. A week later, I drove up a long driveway in the south of France and found Château Feuga.

Sign marking the château's driveway.

I recognized the front door from Margret's photos and had with me a note I found in the archives in Hattiesburg: "We wrote the first CURIOUS GEORGE in 1939 in the tower of an old castle—then owned by friends of ours . . ."

Château Feuga, present day

The owner and I climbed the dusty old stairs to the only tower that contained a room and took in the same view Hans had all those years ago.

Can you imagine what he thought about while he gazed out this window?

View from Hans and Margret's tower at Château Feuga

CLUE 2
THE TERRASS HOTEL

Again, looking at return addresses and dates on letters, as well as photos, gave me information:

H. A. Rey, Terrass Hotel, 12, Rue de Maistre, Paris 18e.

The Terrass Hotel, present day

Balcony at the Terrass Hotel.

Detectives look at details. When I stayed at the Terrass, I noticed the balconies.

I remembered this photo:

Become a detective. Where is Margret standing? During what season do you think this photo was taken? She is standing on one of the balconies at the Terrass and because there's snow on the ledge, I believe it was winter. She must have been cold out there without her coat.

Here is Hans with Margret's brother, Hans Waldstein.

Do you think this picture was taken in the same place?

I do. And they remembered their coats!

WRITTEN PROOF

Look at this illustration painted by H. A. Rey. Artists often sign and date their work and note the location where they made it. Can you find out when and where he painted this? *Become a detective. Do you see any writing on this painting?*

Illustration from Curious George

Clue 4
Building Blocks

In the archives I found the tiny calendar books Hans kept while the Reys lived in Paris. They helped me construct the timeline of the Reys' journey out of France.

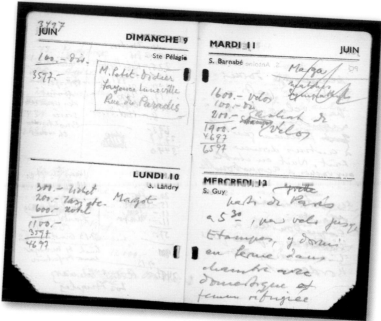

H. A. Rey's diary pages from June 1940.

Become a detective. Hans wrote that they left Paris *par vélo* (by bicycle) for Étampes. *On what day in Juin (June) did they leave?* I can read French, but you could use online translation to read the diary. The note is from Wednesday, June 12. Hans also made a habit of listing their expenses in his diaries. *What did the Reys buy on the days leading up to their escape?* Bicycles, of course! How many French Francs did they cost?

STILL CURIOUS

A few of many questions I would like to ask the Reys if I could.

How did you pack up before leaving France, and how did the Terrass Hotel ship those trunks to America?

What can you tell me about Margret's brother, Hans Waldstein? I know he served in the French Foreign Legion, but I'd like to know more. I love his smile in the photos taken at the Terrass.

What were the exact details of your bicycle and train journey through France, and what was it like at the French border?

Did you walk across the border bridge from Hendaye, France, to Spain, and how did you feel on that day?

What unanswered questions would you like to ask Margret and Hans about their long-ago journey?

ACTIVITIES

1. Make a Timeline

MATERIALS:

sheets of copy paper, markers or pencils, tape, ruler

- Make a list of events in the Reys' lives.
  Here are some events—look through the book and
  add others of your own:

1906	Hans Rey is eight years old, Margret Rey is born.
1925	Hans Rey moves to Brazil.
1935	Margret and Hans get married.
1940	The Reys flee Paris.
1941	*Curious George* is published.

- Now make a list of world events that affected the Reys.
  You can find them in the book as well. Here are some to
  start with:

1914	Start of World War I
1918	End of World War I
1939	Start of World War II
1940	German troops enter Paris
1945	End of World War II

Leaving Paris

Etampes

- Tape sheets of paper together to make a long strip. Use the ruler to draw a long line down the center of the strip. Make marks to divide the line into decades from 1900 to 1950. Now divide each decade into ten individual years.
- Add the events to your timeline. You can draw pictures if you want.
- Notice how the events in the Reys' lives relate to the world events.

Through Spain

Portugal

2. Make a Map

MATERIALS:
tracing paper,
markers or pencils,
map of western Europe

- Trace a map that shows France, Spain, and Portugal.

- Locate and mark the cities and towns that are mentioned in this book.

- Using what you learned in the book, draw the Reys' route of escape from Paris to Lisbon.

- You can add dates and pictures if you like.

A Partial Bibliography of Books by
——MARGRET and H. A. REY——

Books by H. A. Rey

Zebrology. London: Chatto & Windus, 1937.

Le Cirque. Paris: Hachette, 1938.

Le Zoo. Paris: Hachette, 1938.

Rafi et les 9 singes. Paris: Gallimard (NRF), [1939].

Raffy and the 9 Monkeys. London: Chatto & Windus, 1939.

Anybody at Home? London: Chatto & Windus, 1939.

Au Clair de la Lune and Other French Nursery Songs.
New York: Greystone Press, 1941.

Curious George. Boston: Houghton Mifflin, 1941.

How Do You Get There? Boston: Houghton Mifflin, 1941.

Cecily G. and the 9 Monkeys. Boston: Houghton Mifflin, 1942.

A Christmas Manger: A New Kind of Punch-Out-and-Play Book.
Boston: Houghton Mifflin, 1942.

Elizabite: Adventures of a Carnivorous Plant.
New York & London: Harper & Brothers, 1942;
Boston: Houghton Mifflin, 1999.

Uncle Gus's Circus: A New Kind of Cut-Out-and-Play Book.
Boston: Houghton Mifflin, 1942.

Uncle Gus's Farm: A New Kind of Cut-Out-and-Play Book.
Boston: Houghton Mifflin, 1942.

Tommy Helps, Too. Boston: Houghton Mifflin, 1943.

Where's My Baby? Boston: Houghton Mifflin, 1943.

Feed the Animals. Boston: Houghton Mifflin, 1944.

Curious George Takes a Job. Boston: Houghton Mifflin, 1947.

Curious George Rides a Bike. Boston: Houghton Mifflin, 1952.

The Stars: A New Way to See Them. Boston: Houghton Mifflin, 1952.

Find the Constellations. Boston: Houghton Mifflin, 1954.

See the Circus. Boston: Houghton Mifflin, 1956.

Curious George Gets a Medal. Boston: Houghton Mifflin, 1957.

Curious George Learns the Alphabet. Boston: Houghton Mifflin, 1963.

The Original Curious George. Boston: Houghton Mifflin, 1998.

BOOKS BY MARGRET AND H. A. REY

How the Flying Fishes Came into Being. London: Chatto & Windus, 1938.

Pretzel. New York: Harper & Brothers, 1945; Boston: Houghton Mifflin, 1997.

Spotty. New York: Harper & Brothers, 1945; Boston: Houghton Mifflin, 1997.

Curious George Flies a Kite. Boston: Houghton Mifflin, 1958.

Curious George Goes to the Hospital. Boston: Houghton Mifflin, 1966.

The Complete Adventures of Curious George. Introduction by Madeleine L'Engle. Afterword by Margret Rey. Boston: Houghton Mifflin, 1994.

Whiteblack the Penguin Sees the World. Boston: Houghton Mifflin, 2000.

The Complete Adventures of Curious George. Introduction by Leonard S. Marcus. Retrospective Essay by Dee Jones. Boston: Houghton Mifflin, 2001.

Curious George and Friends: Favorite Stories. Introduction by Margaret Bloy Graham. Boston: Houghton Mifflin, 2003.

Billy's Picture. New York: Harper & Brothers, 1948; Boston: Houghton Mifflin, 2004.

BOOKS ILLUSTRATED BY H. A. REY

Don't Frighten the Lion! by Margaret Wise Brown. New York: Harper & Brothers, 1942.

The Park Book by Charlotte Zolotow. New York: Harper Books, 1944.

Katy No-Pocket by Emmy Payne. Boston: Houghton Mifflin, 1944.

IMAGE CREDITS

Library of Congress, Prints & Photographs Division, Photochrom Collection: pages 10 (foreground left: LC-DIG-ppmsca-00415; foreground right: LC-DIG=ppmsca-00424; background: LC-DIG-ppmsca-00419), 12 (LC-DIG-ppmsca-00404), 32 (background: LC-DIG-ppmsc-05136)

H.A. & Margret Rey Papers, de Grummond Children's Literature Collection, The University of Southern Mississippi: title page (right), 4 (top), 6, 7, 8, 9 (left, right), 11 (bottom right), 13 (all), 14 (background), 15 (all), 16 (top left, bottom right), 19 (top right, bottom left), 22 (background), 24 (background), 25 (all), 26 (bottom right), 27 (all), 28 (bottom left), 31 (bottom left), 32 (bottom left), 34 (all), 35, 36 (bottom left), 37 (top right), 38 (right), 39 (top right), 44 (all), 45 (bottom right), 55 (bottom right), 67 (right), 68 (all), 69 (all), 70, 83, 86 (middle and bottom), 88

Bettman/CORBIS: pages 28 (background), 36 (top)

Hulton-Deutsch Collection/CORBIS: pages 22 (bottom), 30 (top)

Underwood and Underwood/CORBIS: page 18

CORBIS: page 39

© 2003 me & my BIG ideasTM: labels on pages 19, 22, 68

Illustrations from *Cecily G. and the 9 Monkeys* by H. A. Rey. Copyright 1942, and copyright © renewed 1969 by H. A. Rey. Reprinted by permission of Houghton Mifflin Company. All rights reserved.

Illustrations from *Curious George* by H.A. Rey. Copyright 1941, and copyright © renewed 1969 by Margret E. Rey. Copyright assigned to Houghton Mifflin Company in 1993. Reprinted by permission of Houghton Mifflin Company. All rights reserved.

Illustration by H.A. Rey from *Katy No-Pocket* by Emmy Payne. Copyright 1944 by Houghton Mifflin Company. Copyright © renewed 1972 by Emmy Govan West. Reprinted by permission of Houghton Mifflin Company. All rights reserved.

Illustrations from *Whiteblack the Penguin Sees the World* by Margret and H.A. Rey. Copyright © 2000 by Lay Lee Ong. Reprinted by permission of Houghton Mifflin Company. All rights reserved.

Illustrations from *Au Claire de la Lune and Other French Nursery Songs*. Copyright © 1941 by H.A. Rey, Greystone Press. Copyright © renewed 1991 by the Rey Estate. Reprinted by permission of the Rey Estate.

Louise Borden: pages 84–85, 86 (top)

LOUISE BORDEN is the author of thirty books for young readers, both fiction and nonfiction, including *Across the Blue Pacific,* illustrated by Robert Andrew Parker, and *His Name Was Raoul Wallenberg.* Her subjects range from kindergarten to baseball to World War II. Louise and her husband, Peter, have three grown children and live in Cincinnati, Ohio.

ALLAN DRUMMOND studied illustration at the Royal College of Art in London and has lived and worked in France and the United States.